# BIRMINGHAM IN THE 70s AND 80s

Alton & Jo Douglas

*Best Wishes Alton & Jo Douglas*

The city's famous King Kong statue dominates the scene in Manzoni Gardens, 11th May 1972. For a while it resided in a Camp Hill used car site but for several decades now has been in Scotland and Cumbria.

ISBN 978-1-85858-511-6
Published by Brewin Books Ltd, Doric House, 56 Alcester Road, Studley, Warwickshire B80 7LG.
Printed by Gomer Press Limited.
Layout by Alton and Jo Douglas.

The Queen is greeted outside the Council House by the crowds during part of her Silver Jubilee tour, 27th July 1977.
The Lady Mayoress is Coun Freda Cocks OBE.

Front Cover: Corporation Street, 15th August 1986.

# Contents

# BREWIN BOOKS LTD

Doric House, 56 Alcester Road,
Studley, Warwickshire, B80 7LG
Tel: 01527 854228  Fax: 01527 852746
VAT Registration No. 705 0077 73

*Dear Nostalgic,*

*By combining these decades we hope that we've managed to convey the hustle and bustle of a rapidly changing world. As usual there are well over 300 images with, once again, a predominance of the type of street scenes so many of you love (always the most popular feature in our books). The 70s were an eventful time for the BBC with the last days of Broad Street, the opening of Pebble Mill and the Corporation's 50th Anniversary. The theatres were extremely busy and we've tried to represent, as much as possible, the professional and amateur activities. For some reason we're all addicted to trawling through old advertisements (the second most popular components) so you'll find plenty of evidence that, amongst other things, we always have been "a nation of shopkeepers". Incidentally, if you think that the 80s were too recent to be included in a "Nostalgic" collection just bear in mind that they came to an end almost a quarter of a century ago!*

*One personal confession that reveals the exhibitionist side of my nature. I could not resist the temptation to finish with a marching band. So, join the parade as we once more beat the drum for our city.*

*Yours, in friendship,*

Alton

The City Museum and Art Gallery, May 1984.

3

# THE 70s

Sarehole Mill, at the junction of Wake Green Road and Cole Bank Road, Hall Green, 1970.

4

Closing down sale at Snape's, Great Hampton Street, 1970.

The booking hall is just about recognisable as the old Snow Hill Station is dismantled, 1970. A temporary entrance was made, in Livery Street, to allow for the limited service still in operation.

Temple Row, 1970.

Gas Street Basin, 1970.

Junior soldiers, from the Sutton Coldfield Fusiliers, take part in the National Canal Boat
Rally, Gas Street Basin, c1970.

Football training under floodlights, Shard End Community Centre,
Packington Avenue, 1970.

Singer, Eartha Kitt, appearing at the Hippodrome,
9th November 1970.

The control room and studio ready for a recording
of "The Archers", BBC, Broad Street, 1971.

One of the last remaining workshops,
AB Row/Gem Street, 1971.

Coventry Road, with Langley Road on the right, Small Heath, 14th February 1971.

Union Street, 1971.

A music lesson given by Mrs D Bennett, Woodlands Hospital Special School, 24th June 1971.

Interval entertainment from the Hy-Kells, St. Andrews, 1971.

Congregational Church, Grove Lane, Handsworth, September 1971.

The traditional "topping out" ceremony by the team building the Evening Mail
show house, Midlands Ideal Home Exhibition, Bingley Hall, 9th September 1971.

Princess Anne opens the new BBC Pebble Mill Studios, 10th November 1971. With her are Music Producer, Michael Ford (L) and Radio Network Editor, Jock Gallagher.

Miners from Staffordshire and South Wales arrive to join the pickets in the dispute with the West Midlands Gas Board, 10th February 1972. It became known as The Battle of Saltley Gate.

The last train leaves Snow Hill Station, 4th March 1972.

Victorian urinals, Oaklands Park, Yardley, 1972.

13

The annual Lucas Sports Day, Witton, 1972.

Glenavon Road, Kings Heath, 25th August 1972.

Camden Street School, Brookfields, 1972.

Camden Street School, Brookfields, under demolition, 25th August 1972.

The Kingston cinema, now a Bingo Hall, Coventry Road/Kingston Road, Small Heath, 1972.

Bordesley Park Road/Coventry Road, Small Heath, 1972.

Aldridge Road/Queslett Road, Perry Barr, 16th October 1972.

Elizabeth Queenan poses for members of Shard End
Community Centre Photographic Club, November 1972.

# 50TH ANNIVERSARY OF THE BBC

BRITISH POST OFFICE MINT STAMPS

Cherry Street, 1973.

Coventry Road with Green Lane on the right, 1973.

Temple Row/Cherry Street, 1973.

The Chester Peterson Combo with Avis St Clare, Winners of the Evening Mail talent competition, East Birmingham Trades and Labour Club, Highfield Road, Alum Rock, May 1973.

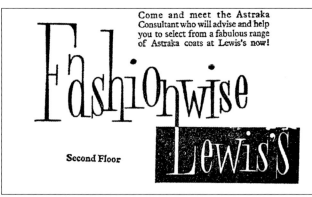

The Duke of Edinburgh, Hooper Street/Dudley Road, Springhill, 15th June 1973.

High Street, 1973.

Lewis's staff hold a meeting to voice their dissatisfaction with the proposed Christmas working hours, December 1973.

Lord Fowler of Sutton Coldfield

Elected MP for Sutton Coldfield in 1974, the year it became part of the city of Birmingham  and continued until his elevation to the House of Lords in 2001.

Sir Peter Scott, probably best known as a distinguished ornithologist, is installed as Chancellor of the University of Birmingham, May 1974. He held the post until 1983.

Erdington District Postal Office, 1974. Hugh "Lofty" Crawford sits on the left, accompanied by Ron Coleman.

High Street, with Barnabas Road on the right, Erdington, 1974.

Blue Peter, Bromford Bridge, October 1974.

Prince Albert Street, Bordesley Green, 1974.

Bristol Road, Selly Oak, 27th November 1974.

BBC "Pebble Mill At One" presenters, Bob Langley and Donny McCleod and their guest Christine Brewer, proudly sport Aston Villa's colours, December 1974. It was an item, on the programme, displaying the club's centenary goblets – described as "The ultimate in soccer souvenirs".

The Mason Lounge, Arts Building, University of Birmingham, c1975.

Yew Tree Primary School
CERTIFICATE

AWARDED TO *Julie Dillon*

FOR *achieving six merit awards in Class 5.*

DATE *17/2/75.* _____ HEADTEACHER

Alcester Road, Moseley, 15th June 1975.

THIRTY young Birmingham children today helped Mr. Denis Howell, Minister for Sport and Recreation, to launch the first National Tree Planting week.

The children, all from Nechells Primary School, Eliot Street, Nechells, helped to plant 25 Sycamore trees on an open site at the junction of Priory Road and Aston Hall Road, Aston.

THE QUEEN received a warm welcome when she landed in freezing snow at Birmingham Airport today for the prestige official opening of the National Exhibition Centre.

More than 100 Union Jack waving school children cheered when the Queen and the Duke of Edinburgh came down the steps of the Royal plane at Elmdon.

2.2.76

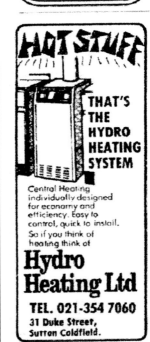

Hob Moor Road Community Centre, Small Heath, 1976. Now part of Starbank Road School.

The remnants of the old Snow Hill Station, 1976.

Cambridge Street canal development, c1976.

Steam Traction Engine, Sports Day, Oaklands Park, Yardley, 1976.

Talbot (Singer) Works, Coventry Road, Small Heath, 1976.

Part of the opening ceremony, at the new home of the Birchfield Harriers, Alexander Stadium, Perry Park, 1976.

Icknield Street, Hockley, c1976.

Union Street, 29th December 1976.

Temple Row, 1977.

Navigation Inn, Tyburn Road, Erdington, c1977.

As part of the Queen's Silver Jubilee celebrations she presents new colours to the 2nd Battalion Mercian Volunteers, Broad Street, 27th July 1977.
The Queen can be seen circled below.

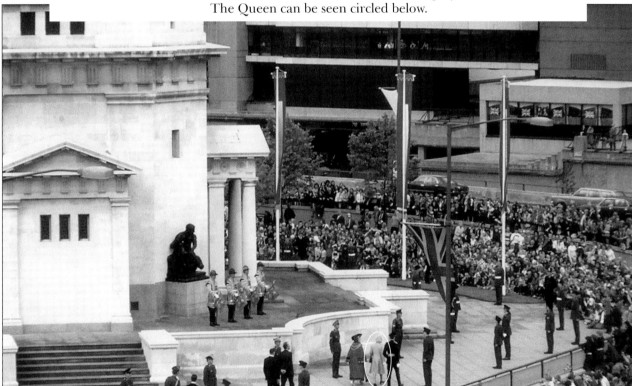

**Birmingham Triennial Musical Festival**

ON THE OCCASION

of

THE SILVER JUBILEE

of

H.M. QUEEN ELIZABETH II

TOWN HALL

Presented by the City of Birmingham in association with the
Arts Council of Great Britain

The Jewellery Quarter, 1977.

Mary Cox retires after 42 years at The Crown,
Broad Street, 1977.

St Cyprian's, The Fordrough, Coventry Road, Hay Mills, 1977.

## HANDSWORTH PHOTOGRAPHIC SOCIETY

This Society exists to develop the enjoyment of photography as a creative hobby, and all interested are invited to attend the lectures, which should prove of practical assistance to them.

The Society meets each Wednesday at Headquarters, and meetings commence at 7.45 p.m. Whenever possible, after a lecture, opportunity will be given for print criticism, and members are invited to bring their work along for this purpose.

### ANNUAL SUBSCRIPTIONS

Gentlemen £2.50, Ladies and Juniors 50p may be paid direct to the Treasurer

Members £2.50     Man and Wife £3
Juniors and Senior Citizens 50p

### COMPETITIONS

PRINTS to have the class, title and name of entrant written on the back of the mount. SLIDES to be mounted between glass, spotted with a single spot in the left-hand bottom corner when the slide is viewed as it is to appear on the screen, and marked with the title and name of entrant. Slides should also be entered together with a completed entry Prints and/or Slides must be handed in by dates stipulated.

## HANDSWORTH PHOTOGRAPHIC SOCIETY

President :
N. B. HARVEY

Vice-Presidents :
F. W. REA          J. R. HURLEY

## WINTER PROGRAMME 1977/8

•

Headquarters :
FRIENDS' HALL, FARM STREET
BIRMINGHAM 19

Small Heath Baptist Church, Coventry Road/Jenkins Street, c1978.

Oldknow Road School, Small Heath, 1978.

## AMATEUR SWIMMING ASSOCIATION
## ENGLISH SCHOOLS' SWIMMING ASSOCIATION

### SPEED SWIMMING AWARD
### MERIT

May 1978

Julie Dillon

The Committees of the Amateur Swimming Association and the English Schools' Swimming Association wish to congratulate you upon your achievement in gaining the above award for style and speed swimming.

The badge which you are entitled to wear is enclosed herewith and we hope that you will continue to make progress and derive much pleasure from your swimming.

Yours faithfully,

Organiser.

# WEST HEATH CARNIVAL 1978

### SATURDAY 17th JUNE

**WEST HEATH RECREATION GROUND STAPLELODGE ROAD**

**PROGRAMME 10p**

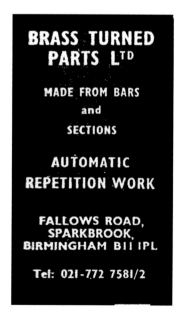

BBC researcher, Keith Ackrill, meets with Cliff Richard and EMI record representative, Julia Griffiths, at a reception given by her company, Albany Hotel, 27th September 1978.

The Dutch Swing College Band, "Pebble Mill At One", BBC, 6th February 1979.

The Carlton Scott Quartet, The Holly Bush, Hagley Road West, Quinton, 1979.

Sutton Coldfield Station, c1979.

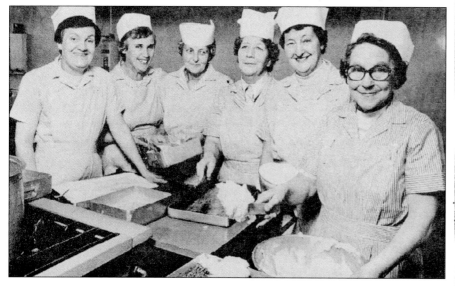

A fire at the Mayfair Suite, Smallbrook Queensway, 26th May 1979.

Dinner ladies, Shirestone School, Tile Cross, 1979.

St Martin's flats, Vaughton Street, Highgate, 13th December 1979.

Tommy Trinder, Jack Tripp and Allen Christie rehearse for "Robinson Crusoe",
Alexandra Theatre, 20th December 1979.

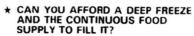

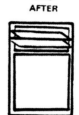
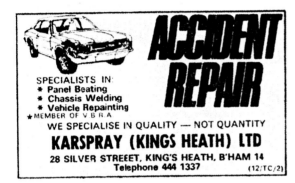

Central Gate, Smithfield Market, Moat Row, 1980.

St Martins Retail Market, 1980.

The new Wholesale Meat Market, 1980.

Horticultural section, Smithfield Market, 1980.

Signalman, Jim Weston, Sutton Coldfield Signal Box, 1980.

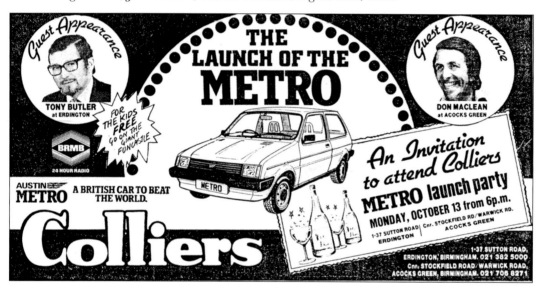

Manager, Ron Saunders, acknowledges the fans' cheers after Aston Villa win the
Football League Championship. Victoria Square, May 1981.

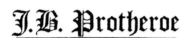

The last days of the Deltic Class, in operation with British Rail, Bromford Bridge, 1981.

The Opposite Lock, Gas Street, 25th February 1982.

Vyse Street/Hylton Street, Aston, 1982.

British Legion Club, Botteville Road, Acocks Green 1982.

*Gillott Road, Edgbaston, 1982.*

Sutton Coldfield Station, Summer 1982. This was a special unit under test but it never came into service.

51

Work on the canal, just off Newhall Street, November 1982.

Corporation Street, looking down towards the Central Fire Station, November 1982.

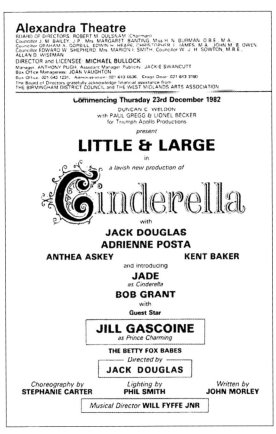

Jack Douglas, Eddie Large and Syd Little, 22nd December 1982.

The Hall of Memory can just be seen through the arches of Paradise Circus, December 1982.
This area is now Paradise Forum.

Celebrating Open Day at Hall Green Little Theatre Victor Price serenades Helen Dawson (left) and Sheila Turner, 27th May 1983. Victor, apart from holding an important position as Alton's uncle, was also the author of several books on Birmingham!

Queensway tunnel, looking towards Holloway Circus, 1983.

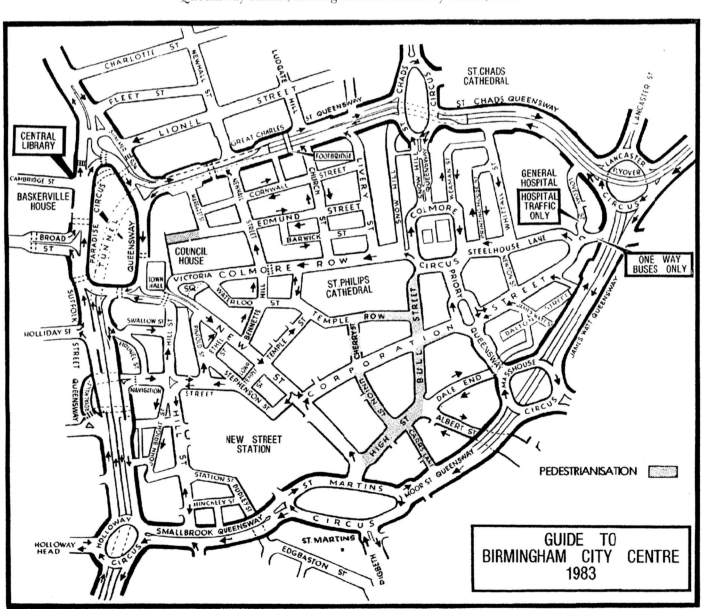

GUIDE TO
BIRMINGHAM CITY CENTRE
1983

St Agnes Church, Pershore Road, Cotteridge, 1983.

Warstone Lane, Jewellery Quarter, 1983.

Cassius Clay shows Dennis Amiss and Bob Willis exactly how the game of cricket should be played, Edgbaston, August 1983.

**Birmingham city centre today received a big blow with the announcement of the closure of yet another large department store — the Co-op in High Street.**

22.11.83

021 373 7586.    021 373 7586.

L·E·G
Leonard oode Ltd.

L·E·G
Leonard oode Ltd.

INDUSTRIAL
AND
COMMERCIAL
PHOTOGRAPHY.

INDUSTRIAL
AND
COMMERCIAL
PHOTOGRAPHY.

**594 COLLEGE ROAD
KINGSTANDING, BIRMINGHAM**

## Alexandra Theatre

BOARD OF DIRECTORS: ROBERT M. OULSNAM (Chairman)
Miss H. N. BURMAN, O.B.E., M.A., Councillor Mrs. T. COOKE,
GRAHAM A. GOPSILL, EDWIN H. HEAPE, CHRISTOPHER J. JAMES, M.A., JOHN M. B. OWEN,
Councillor EDWARD W. SHEPHERD, Mrs. MARION I. SMITH, Councillor W. J. H. SOWTON, M.B.E.,
ALLAN D. WISEMAN, Councillor B. P. ZISSMAN.

DIRECTOR and LICENSEE: **MICHAEL BULLOCK**

Manager: ANTHONY PUGH, Assistant Manager/Publicity: JACKIE SWANCUTT
Box Office Manageress: JOAN VAUGHTON

Box Office: 021-643 1231,  Administration: 021-643 5536,  Stage Door: 021-643 3180

The Board of Directors gratefully acknowledge financial assistance from
THE BIRMINGHAM DISTRICT COUNCIL

**Commencing Monday 10th October 1983 — for one week**

PAUL ELLIOTT

*presents*

**MARK MEDOFF'S**

*Children Of A Lesser God*

**ELIZABETH QUINN      RON ALDRIDGE**

*with*

**HOWARD BARNES    CONOR EVANS    SARAH SCOTT
PAMELA MANDELL    KATHERINE HUME**

Settings realised by           Lighting by
ALAN MILLER BUNFORD        JAMES BAIRD

Directed by
**GORDON DAVIDSON**

This production staged by        Associate Producers
Philipa Ailion              Brian Hewitt-Jones
                            Chris Moreno

*Originally produced by the Center Theatre Group, Mark Taper Forum, Los Angeles*

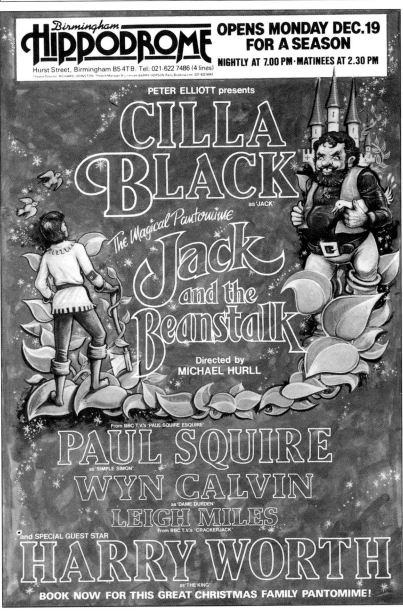

City Arcade, from Union Street, December 1983.

City Arcade, December 1983.

Birmingham Repertory Theatre, Broad Street, April 1984.

Rear of Cambridge Street, April 1984.

Sheepcote Street, Ladywood, 1984.

Stratford Road, from Newton Road, Sparkhill, July 1984.

Broad Street, August 1984.

Broad Street/St Peter's Place, 1984.

King Alfred's Place, off Broad Street, 1984.

Gas Street, 1984. Alton's publicist, George Bartram, had his offices in the top right of the building.

Cumberland Street, 1984.

Oozells Street School, 1984.

An experimental bus track designed to relieve congestion is tested by West Midlands Passenger Transport Executive, 6th August 1984.

Coventry Road, Yardley, September 1984.

*Bournville Musical Society*
(Light Opera Section)
MEMBERS OF THE BOURNVILLE CLUB

*Presents*

# CALAMITY JANE

Music by
SAMMY FAIN
Adapted and Arranged by
RONALD HANMER & PHIL PARK

*Producer:*
BETTY EVANS
*Musical Director:*
JACK MYERS
*Choreographer:*
MAVIS MORRIS
Choreography by BETTY EVANS · "Can-Can" arranged by MAVIS MORRIS
*Coffee will be on sale during the interval.*

THE CONCERT HALL, BOURNVILLE, 19th-23rd MARCH 1985.

Westley Arms Hotel, Westley Road, Acocks Green, May 1985.

Pop fans queue for tickets in the alleyway, by the Odeon, off New Street, 4th June 1985. It was for a Band Aid concert being staged at Wembley Stadium, a month later, with the proceeds going to Ethiopian famine victims.

# OFFICIAL PROGRAMME

## The British Motoring Festival

**BIRMINGHAM THE BIG HEART OF ENGLAND**

'THE BIG HEART OF THE INDUSTRY'

ORGANISED BY BMIHT AND THE BIRMINGHAM POST & MAIL LTD

## COFTON PARK · LONGBRIDGE · BIRMINGHAM 30 JUNE 1985

### GATES OPEN 10.00a.m.

**OFFICIAL OPENING AT 10.30am. BY NOEL EDMONDS**

Noel Edmonds will arrive by helicopter to perform the official opening and will later compete in the hill climb competition.

### ATTRACTIONS INCLUDE:—

**VETERAN & VINTAGE CLASSIC CAR AUCTION (BY WALTON & HIPKISS)**

**CAR CLUB DISPLAY ● COMMERCIAL VEHICLE DISPLAY**

**MANOEUVRABILITY AND HILL CLIMBING TRIALS ● CONCOURS D'ELEGANCE**
(Sponsored by Classic and Sportscar)

**VINTAGE MOTORCYCLES ● AUTOJUMBLE ● CRAFT FAIR ● AEROBATIC DISPLAY**

**CHILDREN'S AMUSEMENTS PLUS FUN FOR ALL THE FAMILY**

**FREE CAR PARKING**

**PRICE: £1 ADULTS; 50p CHILDREN**

JAGUAR    British Motor Industry Heritage Trust    AUSTIN ROVER

The Birmingham Post Evening Mail Sunday Mercury

Trusthouse Forte Hotels

DUNLOP

Lombard North Central

71

High Street, from Station Road, Harborne, 1985.

C & A Modes, Corporation Street, c1985.

High Street, February 1986.

Woolworth announces it is to close its Bull Ring branch, 1986.

Walmley Road, Sutton Coldfield, c1986. The Fox public house can be seen just beyond the garage.

The Colonnade, Broad Street, 1986. The First World War memorial was relocated to the St Thomas Peace Garden, in Bath Row, in 1995.

Warwickshire's Dennis Amiss leaves the field after scoring his 100th century in the match against Lancashire, Edgbaston, 29th July 1986.

Sarehole Mill, Cole Bank Road, Hall Green, 1986.

The Bull Ring, 1987.

Rehearsal time for the Birmingham Banjo, Mandolin and Guitar Orchestra, Moseley, 1987.

Great Western Arcade, 1987.

Coopers Road, Handsworth, March 1987.

Queuing for butter from the Salvation Army, St Chad's Circus, 23rd March 1987.

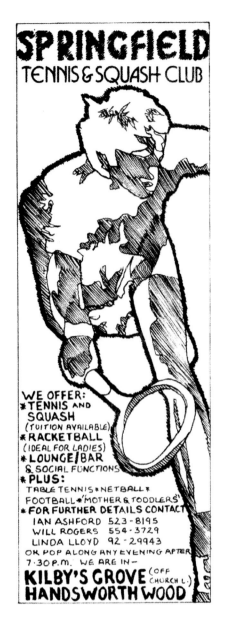

The newly-formed Birmingham Drum and Trumpet Corps. march through Weoley Castle Square, May 1987.

The Committee of the West Midlands Branch of the British Red Cross Society requests the pleasure of your company at
THE COUNCIL HOUSE, BIRMINGHAM
on WEDNESDAY 17th JUNE 1987

to attend the

## ANNUAL GENERAL MEETING OF THE BRANCH

19.00 hrs.  Sherry in the Banqueting Room
19.30 hrs.  Annual General Meeting in the Council Chamber
            Speaker : Mr Stephen Davey (Director Home Division BRCS)
20.30 hrs.  Refreshments in the Banqueting Room

R.S.V.P. Secretary, British Red Cross Society,
34 Blossomfield Road, Solihull,
West Midlands B91 1NS.

Pershore Road, Stirchley, 1987.

Vivian Road/High Street, Harborne, 23rd June 1987.

Spring Lane/Fern Road, Erdington, August 1987.

This was a charity walk from Moor Street to
Snow Hill Station, 12th September 1987.

The Queen Mother receives a bouquet from George Bache shortly after opening the Law Courts, 18th November 1987.

The Green, Kings Norton, 1988.

The Bulls Head, The Green, Kings Norton, 1988.

The Parade, Sutton Coldfield, 1989.

BIRMINGHAM CATHEDRAL

A CIVIC SERVICE

FOR THE

CENTENARY OF THE CITY

1889~1989

Saturday 14th January 1989 at 11.00 am

CITY OF BIRMINGHAM CENTENARY FESTIVAL

1889 1989

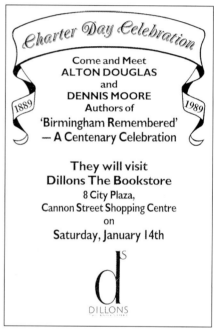

Charter Day Celebration

Come and Meet
ALTON DOUGLAS
and
DENNIS MOORE
Authors of
'Birmingham Remembered'
— A Centenary Celebration

1889    1989

They will visit
Dillons The Bookstore
8 City Plaza,
Cannon Street Shopping Centre
on
Saturday, January 14th

d s
DILLONS

Part of the new-look Birmingham underway, with traffic going along Broad Street on the left,
by the Hall of Memory, 1989.

Steam Traction Rally, Science Museum, Newhall Street, 1989.

The West Midlands Police Band take part in the Lord Mayor's Parade, New Street, 27th May 1989.

Back Cover: Moseley Road, Moseley c1970.

## ACKNOWLEDGEMENTS

(for providing photographs, encouragement and numerous other favours)

Keith Ackrill; Norman Bailey; The Birmingham City Council Dept. of Planning and Architecture; The Birmingham Post and Mail Ltd; Roy Dillon; Christine Grainger; Albert Holmes; Dave, Thelma and Tom Jones; Vernon Jones; Paul Kelsall; Brian Matthews; Alfred Miller; Dennis Moore; Network West Midlands; David Parkes; David Parsons; Wendy Payne; John Pierce; Bernard Robbins; Peter Robinson; Fred Robinson; Keith and Stella Price; Keith Shakespeare; Margaret and Arthur Smith; Roger Smith; Cynthia Thomas; Sid Turnbull; Mary Turner; University of Birmingham; Brian Webb; Rosemary Wilkes; Keith Williams; Ken Windsor.

Please forgive any possible omissions. Every effort has been made to include all organisations and individuals involved in the book.

Happiness at Yew Tree Primary School, Aston, Summer 1977. They were just about to set off for a field trip to Belbroughton.

88